A Ribbon of Broken Colors*

* I've used the image of ribbons of broken colors as a cover and as the title for my memoirs. Autism has taken on many different aspects during during my life, intertwining itself in my daily living.

A Ribbon of Broken Colors

Growing up a square peg in a round world.

MARK THOMPSON

A RIBBON OF BROKEN COLORS
GROWING UP A SQUARE PEG IN A ROUND WORLD.

iUniverse books may be ordered through booksellers or by contacting:

iUniverse
1663 Liberty Drive
Bloomington, IN 47403
www.iuniverse.com
844-349-9409

Because of the dynamic nature of the Internet, any web addresses or links contained in this book may have changed since publication and may no longer be valid. The views expressed in this work are solely those of the author and do not necessarily reflect the views of the publisher, and the publisher hereby disclaims any responsibility for them.

Any people depicted in stock imagery provided by Getty Images are models, and such images are being used for illustrative purposes only. Certain stock imagery © Getty Images.

ISBN: 978-1-6632-2000-4 (sc)
ISBN: 978-1-6632-2001-1 (e)

Library of Congress Control Number: 2021905817

Print information available on the last page.

iUniverse rev. date: 03/31/2021

My Memoir, Growing up With Autism: a Square Peg in a Totally Round World

Autism makes you seem weird to the world. You desperately want to fit in, but you don't know how. You don't understand why it's so easy for other people. Frustration sets in early, and is a constant companion. This is my story, told from my point of view with some additions from my mother and my wife, Claire.

Intro

Hello, my name is Mark Thompson. I have a mother, father, and an older sibling, to be called OS for this memoir. I am married to a wonderful woman. I have two college degrees, a BA in Sociology from large local university and an AA in Accounting from X Community College. I also have what used to be called Asperger's Syndrome, AS, that term isn't used anymore. I personally don't know what the new term is, so I am going to continue to call what I have AS. It means we are high functioning autistics. People like me, with AS, usually aren't mentally challenged. And we don't look any different than your average person. And most of us aren't like the character in the movie about autistics. What we are is socially challenged big time. I never seemed to fit in with the crowd. Now there is help for sufferers, early testing, early diagnosis and early interventions. There are now teachers that are trained in AS. It is much better understood today. I didn't have that luxury. I wasn't diagnosed until I was a junior in college.

My life was tough, exciting and even boring. Growing up wasn't easy, looking back; I feel that my life was exceptionally hard. Because no one knew what I had, there were no strategies to help me deal with problems. AS people are apt to suffer from anxiety and depression. I knew I was different, I just didn't know how to not be different. Even as an adult I struggle with how to fit in with the rest of the world. The world doesn't understand Autism or Autistics. We are very sensitive and don't take teasing well. I personally have a hard time with criticism. I have a hard time making friends to this day. We tend to fixate on things. In HS, my football teammates noticed I tended to stare at cars. I still love World Wrestling Entertainment, I loved it even back when others preferred WCW. Certain foods make me gag. My parents didn't understand this at all. What I'm going to tell you about my life so far is made up of my opinions and observations. My Mom is going to add her memories too. And when we get to that part of my life, my wonderful wife, Claire, will add her some of her feelings and memories Hopefully this book will be of use to others living with AS, those researching AS, and those who love someone with AS.

Mom

I think this collaboration has been good for both of us. My husband and I had no idea of how difficult life was for Mark. We had no idea moving was such a traumatic experience. We knew there were problems, but we thought we handled things the best we knew how at that time. In our view, we have had a pretty good life. There were never money worries, we could travel, we were able to give the kiddos things above and beyond what is expected, like a stay at home parent, paid for college educations and cars.

Mark

I was born on June XX, 197X, in Arizona. Almost immediately after my birth, my parents rushed back to Saudi Arabia, where they were living at the time. I was born in Arizona where both my Grandmas lived because my parents didn't trust the hospital in Saudi Arabia. I moved 3 times before I was 3. We lived in Saudi Arabia and Maryland. I don't remember those moves. The earliest place I remember is living in Mexico.

Mom

This book was a bit of an eye opener for me. I had no idea how difficult things were for Mark growing up. I did indeed go back to Arizona for Mark's birth. It was a hard decision because it meant our family would be apart for 3 plus months. It wasn't that I didn't trust the hospital in Saudi Arabia, they were very modern, it was that I had no idea which doctor I would be assigned, or even if there would be a doctor available. Our older kiddo, to be called OK by me the rest of this memoir, had been born in, Iran. OK was a fussy baby, ate in drib and drabs, cat napped rather than slept, waned to be near us, but not necessarily held. Mark was totally opposite. He was a cuddly baby. He slept through the night by 6 weeks and was an enthusiastic eater. Life is Saudi Arabia was good. We lived on a compound of cute little prefab houses with other families who worked for the same company. I had the use of a car and driver (women couldn't drive), a mini bus that ran a different route each day that covered all the shopping areas, a swimming pool and lots of company. There were other children for older kiddo, and a preschool. There were other babies for us to be part of a mommy and me group. Mark did everything early, turned over, crept, sat up, crawled, and even walked at 10 months. We didn't encourage any of this, it came naturally. He grew quickly, ate everything with gusto and slept deeply. He did "rock" himself in his crib after being rocked and given last feed. He usually fell asleep quickly. He did make repetitive sounds, like most babies, said mama and da. His first recognizable word however was Kee, kitty, he loved our Siamese cat. It really was a very pleasant time for me. I had household help, friends, decent shopping, husband was one of the managers, and our kiddos were cute and developing normally. I had lots of time to spend with them, and enjoyed it thoroughly.

I'm surprised that Mark doesn't remember our time in Maryland.

We left Saudi when he was 2 for a yearlong state side assignment. It was both fun and trying being back in the States after 5 years in the Middle East. I could drive again. Dad spent much of that year traveling, I enjoyed being a stay at home mom. Both kiddos were in preschool for a few mornings a week so I did get out by myself. I had another mom from our company with two small children who just happened to live on our block. Her husband also traveled. Church is important to us; we found one and both kiddos seemed to enjoy Sunday school. They were both adorable angels in the Christmas pageant. Just before Mark's 3rd birthday, we moved to Mexico.

Mark

I do remember living in Mexico a little. I did go to a preschool every morning. We had a club with a swimming pool and a great play ground that we went to a lot with another family. It was here that my parents noticed I wasn't developing speech normally.

We had live in maids that helped us keep our rooms and toy room picked up, and helped Mom shop.

Mom

I loved living in Mexico. I had two live in maids, a gardener, my own car and several Spanish speaking girlfriends. Life was fun. Dad was assistant country manager. Mark continued to do things early, like riding a two wheel bike with training wheels, like building interesting things with Lego, but wasn't speaking in sentences. The maids weren't English speaking, but we rarely left the kiddos home alone with them unless they were in bed and asleep. Most of the time, we packed up the whole crew and went shopping, to the club, or to a friend's house. The maids like to visit and shop too. Mark's preschool teacher noticed that he still did more parallel play; he didn't interact directly with the other children. We found an English speaking Episcopal Church with Sunday Schools for the kiddos. It was a great help to have a whole community of expats around.

After a year, it was clear that the Mexican government was going through real problems and wasn't doing business with foreign companies like ours. We had a decision to make, take another overseas assignment or go stateside again. We were concerned about Mark's limited speech, so opted for a stateside assignment. I should tell you that I do have a BA in Education, K-8 with teaching minors in Science and Special Ed. I had a gut feeling that there was some sort of learning problem, but had no idea what.

Dad was offered an interesting position with our same company in Virginia, just outside DC. We looked for a home in a great school district, and found one in a VA suburb. It was on a col-de-sac off another col-de-sac, lots of kiddos and stay at home moms, and within walking distance of the elementary school. We really seemed to fit right in. Since it was so safe, the kiddos could play outside almost unattended. All the mothers checked on who was playing in their home, or outside every 15 minutes or so. Mark again went to a 3 morning a week preschool with neighborhood kiddos. OK started 1st grade. That's where we found out that having a great school district doesn't mean getting great teachers. Mark did fine in preschool, OK eventually enjoyed 1st grade.

By the time that Mark was in kindergarten, it was pretty obvious to me that there was some sort of speech problem. The kiddos had always had regular checkups; we knew that Mark's functional hearing and vision were fine. Mark understood things, just didn't always respond verbally. He was still using 2-3 word sentences, and he had to think before he responded. So, we started with his pediatrician. No, everything fine, big healthy boy. He will speak when he is ready. Maybe his OS speaks for him? He finished kindergarten with his teacher suggesting testing for a learning disability.

Very honestly, if anyone had said that Mark was autistic at that time, I wouldn't have had an easy time with the diagnosis. The only autistic children I had ever seen were the severely autistic ones, and they were institutionalized. I had actually been taught in one of my college classes that two things that affected a child's development were the direct fault of the mother. A cold mother caused an autistic child, and over bearing mother caused a homosexual child. I'm pretty sure I wasn't a cold, uncaring mother.

We were in a great county for educational opportunity, so we started the testing cycle. It was not a hit with Mark. He would cry, refuse to do anything, and try to leave the room. I think the testers left a little bit to be desired..... One suggestion was to put him in their summer school program with other "special" children to be evaluated. Sounded good, but Mark was soon bored. They were riding trikes, he rode a two wheeler without training wheels, their swimming was a little inflatable pool, and he could swim in our big, neighborhood pool. He flat out decided he didn't like going. I bribed him with He Man figures. At the end of the summer, the teacher said she had no idea what his placement should be for first grade! She didn't teach in that school district during the regular year and had no idea what our county had for placements. I was not amused. The county would have a few suggestions on school placement, or so she said. We told them we were available all summer except for a week in August. They scheduled and held an IAP meeting for the week we were gone. Unfortunately they never gave us any advance notice of the IAP, we didn't hear about it until after we were back from the beach. I called to see what progress had been made in placement. We were told that they weren't sure as we hadn't responded to the notice of the IAP meeting. They held it without us. (Remember this is in the early '80s, long before internet or cell phones.) I do think this was a bit illegal. In the meantime, Dad had been offered another promotion which meant another move. This time it would be to the Thumb area of Michigan. I didn't even look into schools; I decided they could be much worse than the one we were in.

Mark

We moved a lot when I was young, and I didn't like it at all. I didn't like the testing that was done on me. I didn't like playing soccer. All the kids in my Virginia neighborhood played in a league. My parents made both of us kiddos play in one too.

Mom

One of our favorite Mark isms from that time was from a soccer practice. Practice was over, almost, coach and the herd of boys started running a lap around the track. Except Mark. He sat down and watched ants moving something. Dad told him if he hurried, he could catch up with the group. "Don't worry, Dad", he said, "They'll be back." Can't argue with that logic. Even now, Dad and I occasionally turn to each other and say, don't worry, they'll be back.

Mark

When I was 6, I got into fist fight with a friend that was a year younger than me. I don't remember what it was about. All the neighborhood kids were watching us, cheering the other kid on, even my OS. That hurt. I emerged the victor; I gave the other kid a black eye. Somehow, it made me feel more accepted. His mother heard about it and asked me if I did it. I said yes. The mother said that's not nice, she wasn't hostile, but it hurt me again. Even though I won, I felt that I had done something wrong. I now realize it was wrong to fight, it doesn't solve anything. But, I felt supremacy when I won; I guess that's why people fight.

Mom

I'm going to add in here that Mark never lied, at least not knowingly. I'm not sure if this is true of all AS kiddos, but it certainly is of him. We may have had to dig a bit, ask the right questions, but I personally never remember him telling me an outright lie. A bit different from OS who thought fast on the feet thinker, and had no trouble in telling the truth as OK saw it....

Mark

So, we moved again, from Virginia to Thumb Area, Michigan. It's in what Michiganders the thumb. Two things really stand out in my mind. One was a teacher who made my life miserable; the other was a dog bite.

We lived in a hotel for a month before our home was ready to move into. My OS and I started school commuting from the hotel. I was placed in a "non-determined" classroom. There were 6 other kids, a teacher's aide and a teacher. It just happened to be the school that was in our new subdivision. I had the worst teacher imaginable. I have told you I don't like moving. I like a place to call my permanent, secure residence. I felt that my life was getting stranger and stranger, and I couldn't say how.

The teacher was Mrs. X. She was a special education teacher for the school district. I ended up having her for 1 and 2 grades. People seemed to love her, she got awards and honors. I don't really know if she was good or bad but she definitely wasn't a good match for me. My feeling now is that the district wanted to keep her no matter how bad she was because they really didn't care about the kids in her class. She had a strange way of teaching, there really wasn't much academics taught in her class. I knew my alphabet, and could sound out words because my mom taught me phonetics. Mrs. X. used what she called Apple Sheets. If you got your apple sheet filled up, you got a special privilege. (Mom here, I think most of the special privileges were coloring in a coloring book. This was because her daughter "loved" to do this. Well, Mark didn't. If he could have built something with Lego's, or even had a blank sheet of paper, he might have been ok.) Every time you did a good deed, according to her, you got a star. Most of the stars were for behavior, not academics. If you got an answer wrong, on a sheet, she made you do it again and again. She wouldn't show you where your mistake was, you had to find it for yourself. This was supposed to teach you something, I guess. She wanted you to print everything very neatly and make your letters a certain way. If she didn't like your work, you had to erase it and do it again. There didn't seem to be any reason for this, it was one f★★★★★ up class. I wish I had never been a part of t.

My parents recognized that there was a problem. Since my mother was trained as a teacher, she started with speaking to the teacher first. She asked what seemed to be the problem, since instead of liking school; I started to have stomach aches every morning. That didn't get anywhere. I distinctly remember one day when I really did feel sick during school. I wanted to call home, but I wasn't allowed to because I hadn't finished writing my story. I felt like a caged animal, frantic to leave, Mrs. X even called the principal to make sure I didn't leave until it was time. I really did have some sort of virus and ended up staying home the rest of the week. I wanted to quit school, but of course couldn't because I was too young. That was too bad, because it was only going to get worse. (Mom again, I had not heard about home schooling....)

My parents were starting to have doubts about the school; they spoke with the principal to see if there wasn't some other placement that would be better for me. They had noticed that most of the children in our sub either went to the one parochial school, or they were in AP (advanced placement) classes in other schools. A real problem came when Mrs. X. wanted us to learn to say and write our addresses and phone numbers. My parents always had us learn our new address and phone, just in case. This is way before cell phones and personal computers weren't common. Anyway, Mrs. X. copied my address down wrong from the office. It was 4596 D********, she copied down 4599 D********. I didn't copy down what she wrote on the card because it was wrong. She made me keep doing it and erasing what I wrote over and over. She even called my mother in to say that I was being insubordinate. Mom asked what address Mrs. X had, and told the teacher she had the wrong numbers. Mrs. X. never apologized. This made my parents start looking into other schools. After trying to work with the teacher, and then with the principal, they agreed that this was not the right placement for me. I really hated school. I even started to be afraid of going, not know what awful thing Mrs. X. was going to do that day. My parents started bribing me with toys, 5 good days and I got a present, 4 good days a smaller present, and so on. Somehow I made it through that year.

When my parents found out I was going to have her another year, they tried like hell to get me out of Mrs. X's class. The school fought back with conditions like get testing done; see a child psychiatrist, etc.

All of these would be at my parent's expense. Their theory was that she was a stellar teacher and we should be glad to have her, and moving me would be very harmful to me. In their opinion, of course. It was tearing my family apart; I would have stomach aches I cried myself to sleep at night. My parents were frustrated too; they often yelled at each other and me, it was hell for all of us.

The testing that the district was requiring to even consider moving me took up most of the year. Thinking back, I had had a bad feeling about that school from the very first day. The second year, Mrs. X. wanted us to do essay papers. And if she didn't like the way it was done, she would tell you to do it over. I would write until my hand was sore. There is never any excuse to keep making a student do things over and over. I would get so frustrated that I would cry. Then she would yell at me to stop crying. I remember writing down my numbers, 1-20. Mrs. X said I had 3 numbers backwards. The aide said I had 4. So, which, 3, or 4 numbers backward? She wouldn't tell me, said to figure it out myself. Most teaches try to boost their students confidence, she tried to pull it down. My mother believes now that she got even meaner because we dared to challenge her, the school and the district, and she was taking it out on me. That made me think that all special Ed classes were bad, that they really just wanted the difficult, different kids out of the way.

Another thing I remember distinctly was a field trip towards the end of 2 grade. It was a beautiful May day. The class, 6 kids, was going to one of the student's house for a party. The house was by a river. There was just going to be the one parent, the teacher and the aide. The river is deep and fast, my mom thought that there should be another parent in view of the attraction of the river and tendency for some of the kids to wander. The teacher thought 3 adults was enough. My mom didn't agree, and kept me home. It was on ok day at home, but being by the banks of a river would have been fun too.

My parents were better educated and wealthier that a lot of the people in this town, and finally hired a lawyer and threatened to sue the school district. My parents had done everything they, the school district had asked, but I still ended up staying another whole year with that awful teacher. By law, if the school district couldn't provide the proper safe, educational environment for a student, they had to pay to send the student to the proper placement, even if it's in another school district. . (My parents found out just as we were leaving the Thumb Area, that there was indeed what sounded like better placement in the next county over.) And they were to include parents in IAP meetings. They didn't. The threat of a lawsuit made the difference. They suddenly found the perfect placement, perfect teacher in another school in the district. It was an LD class, 2-3 combined. My mom had to drive me to and from school, but it was so much better. My third grade experience was much better than the other two years. We all really loved that teacher. At the end of 3rd grade, my Dad was offered another promotion, this time in the Detroit area. We had all had such a bad experience with the Thumb Area, we were glad to leave.

My mom did tell me that Mrs. X's family left that summer too. Her husband lost his job with a major car company, which was almost impossible. He found another job, but they would have to relocate. They had the sale of their home fall through at the last minute. And her daughter that the class all had to hear so much about how perfect she was fell off a picnic table and drove splinters into her head. I can't say I was too sorry about the job loss or the sale falling through. I was sorry her daughter got hurt.

Mom

Where to start? VA suburb schools proved to be such a disappointment that moving seemed like a blessing. Mark was speaking more, knew his numbers and letters, and was starting to read I taught the kiddos phonics, whole word approach to reading was the current buzz, but I wasn't sure how good it was by itself. So, a new start in a new school, what could be the harm? The transfers were all with the same company, and always came with a promotion. So, off to Thumb Area, Michigan we went with 2 dogs, 2 cats, 2 parrots, 2 finches, a hermit crab, and 2 kiddos in 2 cars. We looked a bit like a small traveling show. We did indeed live in a hotel for a month. I would drive the kiddos to school, and then go out with the realtor looking at homes around the country club, in what was considered the best area, around what was considered the best elementary school. We finally found and bought a home that had been sitting vacant for a year. I'm not sure why I wasn't shown that home much earlier as we could move in immediately. Our home in Virginia had sold even before we moved. I'm good at moving, so we were in and settled by the middle of October.

I did find it unusual that only one of our neighbors sent their children to our "base" school. The rest went to either the big parochial school, or had advanced placement classes in another school. Wow, just like Lake Woebegone, all the children were exceptional.

At first I liked the school, principal and both kiddos' teachers. OK had no problems fitting in even then was an extrovert in a family of introverts. Since we had a boat load of testing, but no diagnosis, Mark was placed in a non something class. Very small class, great teacher and an aide, we were told. Mark's teacher had a weekly mothers' meeting to discuss plans and problems. Wow, really involved all of us, this is great. I had begun to change my mind in just a few months, Mark wasn't happy. He was unusually a big for his age, easy going kid who seemed to be getting back on what we would consider the right track educationally. So, I started with the teacher. She took it as a person affront that I would even dare question any of her methods.

We were welcomed by some in the Thumb Area, and not by others. My husband's company was merged with a major MI company to update and computerize their systems. Management may have wanted the changes, but the workers and union liked things as they had always been. A grocery clerk told me very rudely "we were taking jobs away from their men". I guess as a group, we seemed to sail in and buy nicer homes in nicer neighborhoods. We were also better educated and horrors of all horrors often drove foreign cars.

I'm not sure that any parent had ever questioned this teacher before, and she didn't much like it. I started out by saying obviously there was some sort of problem, what could we do to work it out? Stonewall. OK, went to the principal. Our son is really unhappy, what can we do? Nothing, she is a wonderful teacher and we should be glad to have her. I was even ready to say she was a good teacher, just not for Mark. Again, stonewall. The school district was no better, they threatened to sue us for child endangerment, we obviously weren't taking proper care of Mark. So, before they would even consider moving him, they had all sorts of requirements. So, testing at U of X, solved nothing, nothing unusual seen except slowness of speech, see a child psychiatrist, who said no problem, checkups from our pediatrician. No problems there either. All this was at our expense.

Early fall of the second year, Mrs. X decided that Mark should be put on Ritalin. Luckily we had a really great pediatrician. He said we should give it a try. But, he said we need to see if Mark really needed it, or did "teacher" need it. So, he said let's start Mark on Ritalin and tell teacher that we are giving it to him and see her how thoughts were as to how it seemed to be helping him. We were also to check to see if we saw a difference in Mark at home. And we were to ask Mark how he felt taking Ritalin. He didn't like taking Ritalin; he said it made him feel funny. Then, the dr. said we would spend Christmas vacation weening him off it, he would have been on it at least 6 weeks by then and if it was going to help him academically, it would have. We were not to tell the teacher we were taking him off Ritalin. If we had a call the first day back from Christmas vacation from teacher asking what happened, we'd know for sure Ritalin was a help. We were then to go until Easter vacation without Ritalin, and then we were to tell the teacher we were going to take Mark off Ritalin. If she called the first day back after Easter break saying he had reverted to his awful ways, then we would know the teacher was the one who thought he needed Ritalin. All January, February, March he was doing just fine according to Mrs. X. Yep, first morning back I had her call, he is awful, you will have to put him back on the drug. Instead, I gave her the doctor's name and number; this was at the doctor's request. I bet he had dealt with this before. . I don't think she ever spoke another civil word to me. I asked for copies of all the testing that the school had done, and for all the written reports. Some were so wrong they made me shiver. Mrs. X thought he was retarded, and would never learn, never read, probably wouldn't graduate HS. Another written report stated that his learning problems obviously stemmed from the fact that he was raised mainly by the non English speaking maids in Mexico?

After we had jumped through all the hoops the district had asked of us and still there was no resolution, we threatened to sue the district. We were then taken seriously, and dog gone, a spot was found in a LD

2-3 combo class at another school in the district. That teacher and her aide made final year there wonderful, even though I now had to drive both kiddos to two different schools, and pick them up. We had OK moved to another school by then too. It was well worth it.

As for Mrs. X, I have never seen a teacher so unprofessional; she talked about the children in front of the children, and was rarely complimentary. She constantly compared her 5 year old daughter with her class. Her daughter was perfect, or course. Her family eventually had a real streak of bad luck. I was sorry about the daughter's injury but not about the job loss or the house sale.

We did look into the parochial school in the thumb area, for both kiddos. It was run by for real nuns who wore habits and wimples. Here we had another Mark ism. After testing, Mark asked me in a loud whisper "if she was a fairy princess"? You have never seen a broader smile than the one on that Sister. She said she had been called many things in her life, but never a fairy princess. That school would have been better; they had a spot for Mark, but not OK. By then I wasn't so pleased with OK's classes either. OK had come to the district a bit ahead of their 3rd class, and loved to read. So, anyone who finished their work early was allowed to read. OK would zoom through things, and then read. Same thing happened in the 4th grade class. OK only did what to be done to do to make a good grade, and then spent time reading. We had OK tested, and dog gone, OK qualified for the AP class in a different school. OK didn't care for that at first because there was work involved to keep up. Eventually OK settled in and liked it a bit better.

We had both kiddos play seasonal team sports; Mark never liked any of them. We thought it would be good for them. He did have a good friend, his first, in the Thumb Area. They actually played together, usually He Man. We had every He Man figure, and all the accoutrements that went along with the He Man figures.

When Dad was offered a promotion in the Detroit area, same company, we gladly moved. At least 3 of us gladly moved. Mark still didn't like change at all. One thing I did do properly for him, both kiddos actually was to keep all their toys and set up their rooms the same in each new home. It was their decision when to get rid of things.

We don't have good memories of the Thumb Area as a whole. I had started to doubt myself as a mother, what did I do wrong for Mark to have been so unhappy? I ate and drank way too much and managed to gain 50 pounds in 3 years. I see now that I was very depressed.

I noticed that he forgot to say anything about the dog bite. He bent over and scared our Chow, Osa, when she was asleep. She jumped up and bit hard, he had to have stitches. We found another home for Osa with our Vets help. That was a hard decision, but had to be.

Mark

When I was 9, we moved to a Detroit area suburb where I spent the next 10 years of my life. Out of all the places where I lived, I guess Detroit is pretty much home. Even to this day, I tell people I am from Detroit.

My family joined an Episcopal church. I admit I didn't always like it, the services usually ran 1 ½ hours, sometimes even 2 hours. My family had a more formal taste in worship; I had more casual taste in religion. I did have respect for the Episcopal Church growing up, but I lost that respect at some point. I will discuss that later.

Mom

I'm not sue why the theological discussion here, he was a kid; he went to church with his family. He seemed to really like going to youth group Sunday evenings.

Mark

I have to say that not everything about the way my parents brought me up was good. My father was a believer in corporal punishment. He always said he didn't enjoy spanking me, but I find that hard to believe to the present day. I mean, why would he spank me when most researchers say parents shouldn't spank their children period? They believe it teaches that it is ok to bully people and ok to use violence to solve problems. I find that plausible because my OS loved to hit and fight with me a lot. I met kids on the playground that said their parents spanked them and you can bet your bottom dollar that they enjoyed fighting. My father would even say to me it was wrong to hit others. It has been proven that children pay more attention to what parents do than what they say. And even researchers that agree with corporal punishment believe that you shouldn't use foreign objects like belts or wooden spoons. And they recommend only two swats. They also feel that parents should never hit out of anger. I feel that my parents did all of those things. And punishment should only be used for rotten behavior, not accidents. I remember my father spanking me because I accidently let the dog out. She snuck out behind me. My father knew it was an accident, but he spanked me anyway. And I am not the kind of person that takes spankings well. In fact, it made me want to hit them back. People would say that that is disrespecting your parents, but I feel hitting your child isn't respectful either. I call that parental arrogance. It even goes against what the bible teaches in Ephesians 6:4 "Ye parents provoke not your children to wrath, but bring them up in the nature and admonition of the Lord". So I thought that my parent was a hypocrite. I don't think Jesus likes hypocrisy. If you really read the bible, you will see that there is no reason for hypocrisy ever. I don't believe corporal punishment even teaches morality. It just made me mad and vindictive. And control doesn't teach children cognitive skills, or right from wrong. It only makes people more crazy and paranoid. If all you want is mere control and no true intellectual thought, maybe you should move to a fascist society, a free society isn't for you. My father stopped punishing me when I was 13. I had just micowaved a pizza in the basement rec room and got grease on the floor. I often stained the floor. He just went insane, and told me to bend over. I said no. It was a war of wills, but I was stronger. I have no regrets to this day that I stood up to what I believed no corporal punishment. He did try to spank me again a few months later, I said no again. He lectured me that I must obey the law and my parents. He never tried to spank me again.

I also didn't like the way that my father would just eat my food out of the refrigerator without asking my permission. My mother would lecture me that it was wrong to let food spoil. I personally would rather have had the food spoil than someone eating it behind my back.

Mother

Once again, this surprised me. I do remember spanking, and yes, even with a wooden spoon. I don't remember us "beating" our kiddos. And it was usually over something fairly major. Of course, Mark and I remember things from a different prospect. Mark has/had an unusually accurate memory. We used to call him professor because he would remember an event perfectly and lecture us on it. I'm sorry if he feels that we were too liberal with punishment. We did what we felt was needed at the time. And, we didn't understand that because of the AS, Mark perceived things differently. Sorry kiddo, we can't go back and undo things. You notice that he said he let the dog out by accident. It probably was an accident. That dog was a runner, and could play" keep away" for quite a long time. This meant two of us had to try and catch her. Mark often seemed in a fog about his environment. By that I mean he didn't always notice things around him, like a dog about to escape. And he seems truly surprised that Dad would react to spilling food on the carpet. Our kiddos had their own rooms. We also had half of our large basement refinished as a rec room for the kiddos in the Detroit area home. We put in durable carpet, paneling, a snack kitchen (fridge and microwave, sink, cabinets, counters) full bath, heating and cooling. There was a big TV for games, Betamax player, small foosball table and pin ball machine. It was a really nice place for the kiddos; we spent quite a bit of money on it. It really annoyed me when things were spilled and not cleaned up, or dishes left in the sink for days.

It also surprises me that Mark is still upset about "his" food being taken. He didn't buy it. It usually was something left over from a dinner out, fast food, pizza etc. Dad is bad about just rummaging in the fridge and taking what looks good, regardless of whose food it was originally. I don't remember Mark having a problem eating all the chips, or cookies.

Mark was a bit of a picky eater at this time, used to drive me up a wall. He liked chicken, rice, noodles, apples, oranges, bananas, peanut butter, bread, V8 juice, orange juice, milk, yogurt, cereal and that's about it. No veggies or salads, didn't care for beef or pork. He would tell us that certain foods filled him up too fast. He could throw up at will, it seemed. We now know that AS people do have food sensitivities, and that things can make them physically ill. But any fast food was inhaled with gusto. His picky eating started at about age 4. Up until then, he ate everything. When he was about 15, he decided to start trying thigs again, so ate salads, discovered sushi, most veggies and was willing to try different things. He was always big for his age, so I didn't worry about him getting a "proper" diet.

He is a picky ish eater to this day, but he is willing to try almost anything new.

Mark, Detroit area continued

I started playing soccer again and just hated every minute of it. I remember I would be doing a lot of running and I would get bad cramps and had sore feet after practice. In the early days, I never got to play the position I wanted. I felt that half back would be the best position for me because I like to move around a lot. Coach wanted me to play full back where I would be covering just half the field. I did not enjoy spring soccer all. I didn't want to play again in the fall, but unfortunately my mom signed me up. At first she said I didn't have to play if I didn't want to. At the last minute, she told me I had to play. I felt I wasn't good at soccer and I don't like to run, unless I'm playing a position I like. I hated being confined to just a part of the field. And yes, I was out of position a lot. But for some strange reason, I liked just running around. I do remember that coach would tell me I wasn't following the rules. He would even yell at me to do something else. I wasn't respected by my team mates at all. They would laugh at me. There was another boy who wasn't popular with the team either, he loved to laugh at me too. Maybe he thought that would make him more popular. Boy was he wrong. There was one teammate who I did like and he would explain the other teammates to me. I wish he had gone to my school. Sometimes on the field, my brain just wouldn't act right. Instead of running, I would skip. People told my parents only girls skipped! Later I did get to play the position I wanted, but it didn't make my attitude toward the sport any better. I was not having fun, and I didn't like it one bit.

I also remember how hurt I was at the end of the year soccer party. I was a 4th grader. It was at a local pizza parlor. My parents both came, however they told me we would all have to leave after 1 hour. I was pulled away even though I was having fun and would have liked to play some of the arcade games. My OS had a birthday party to go to at about the same time. I was willing to stay there alone and wait for them after they dropped off OS at that party on the other side of town. To this day I feel that I was deprived of a social interaction with my teammates. We did have pizza for dinner that evening to try make up for having to leave early. I don't think that they understood that it didn't make up for leaving. I was having fun and the fact that I didn't enjoy soccer in the first place; they just didn't take my feelings into consideration. I felt that soccer wasn't right for me, and I never played it gain, except in school gym classes.

Mom

Mark doesn't seem to understand that our time was divided between both our kiddos. Dad often got tied up in business calls even on the weekends, so we didn't like to rely on him being available for any kiddo transportation. This was the eighties; cellphones were just getting to be used by people. They were extremely expensive, a family had one, not one for each person in the family, so leaving kiddos places wasn't really an option. Neither one of our kiddos is really athletic, OK enjoyed sports for the social aspect, Mark didn't enjoy any of it. We had thought that it might help him make more friends. He did have a friend in our new neighborhood. Both boys had a whole lot of popular toys, and spent hours together. Unfortunately, they moved after 2 years.

This was a good/bad time for us. Dad's career was growing; we had lot benefits because of that, beautiful home, nice cars, a swimming pool, and great vacations. Also because of that, I was the primary parent, the one who had to juggle the kiddos' school, after school activities, transportation, homework and the like. I made really good friends there, had an enviable life but was severely depressed. I became more depressed because I felt I really didn't have reason to be depressed. I continued to eat and eventually gained 100 pounds. I hated myself for being so obese, but couldn't seem to get a handle on losing weight. I'm also very affected by light, now know that is called SAD. Michigan in the winter isn't good for natural light; I remember gray skies for months at a time. I also don't care for cold. So, gray and cold, no wonder why I only have a few great memories of Detroit. Dad's mother died while we were in there. It made me realize that our parents had grown old, and we were half a country away from them. (The kiddos only had Grandmas; both Grandpas had died very young before they were born.) The summers there were short and usually beautiful, and the falls were spectacular. The winters are cold, gray and go on forever.

After dealing with several doctors, I was finally tested for a thyroid problem. Previous doctors just wanted me to take antidepressants. I was obese, and most doctors thought I was looking for an easy fix with a thyroid excuse. Well, I really did have a thyroid problem, and one small pill helped most things. I was no longer depressed, no longer wanted to over eat and drink, didn't feel cold as badly and didn't have horrendously dry skin and hair. The one thing it didn't do was help with the weight. Oh well, At least I knew why I had been so depressed.

Mark

Well, for three years I went to the local base school. Because of my bad years with Mrs. X, I started back in the 3rd grade. I found that humiliating. My years with that awful teacher, Mrs. X, really hurt my education progress. To my knowledge, it is very rare for a student to be held back a grade, just another consequence of having a really bad teacher I guess, it's unfair. My mother adored my 3rd grade teacher; she thought she was a really great teacher. I loved her too. I really remember the time I starred in the 3rd grade play. I was the "Mighty Germ". People thought I was a really good actor. Well, I guess that is something to be proud of. Unfortunately, the next year things went downhill again.

Mom

I didn't realize Mark thought it was humiliating to start back in 3rd grade at his new school, in a new town. We did try to talk him through the fact that he hadn't failed; he just would have had a hard time to go directly into 4th grade. We tried to make him see that it was a fresh start, new town, new school. He had a wonderful teacher the last year in the Thumb Area, but that didn't make up for two really bad academic years. Personally, I don't think it is rare for concerned parents to hold a child back a year. He did get an exceptionally good 3rd grade teacher. She took a chance giving him the starring role in the play. He kept that a secret from us and learned his lines himself. He gave a fantastic performance, no stage fright, said his lines with real feeling. I was so proud of him.

Mark

As I said, things started to go bad again in 4th grade. I began hanging with the bad boys of the 4t and 5th grades. I wanted to be in their club. I was very naïve. I can't tell you how much living with AS sucks. At first, I thought I was a leader. They wanted me to engage in a deed that still haunts me. They wanted me to grad a girl's ass. I didn't know that that would be sexual harassment. I realize now that it certainly was. The girl told the playground supervisor. I told the supervisor that the 5th grade boys told me to do it. I can't deny that I wanted to be thought of as cool. Doesn't just about everybody want to be cool? But at what price? This went to the assistant principal; here I will admit I lied. I told her that the boys would beat me up if I told on them. I don't think they could have because I didn't live in their neighborhood. They did admit that they asked me to grab the girl's ass. We all had to miss one recess. I guess the disciplinary action could have been much worse. After that, I decided to not hang with them in the What's up, What's up Club. That's what they called themselves. So, to become cool, I became a fool. To this day, I preach that it's better to be dumb than naïve. Being naïve can really screw up your life. This was one of the incidents in my life that inspired me to keep up with what's going on in this world. I want to know exactly what's going on all the time. Now I use a website started in the 21 century called Realclearpolitics.com to keep up with all headlines. There are people who think I keep up with headlines too much and that this is causing anxiety in my life. I just want to see what's going on, what the world is coming to. I really want to come across as a person who is well educated, not a person who is s★★t brained or naïve.

Mom

I was never contacted about that incident. Too bad maybe I could have intervened earlier. What I remember most is that Mark got good grades, studied for tests, really took school seriously. What I also distinctly remember is that Mark had three pairs of glasses broken by the same boy at his school; all were "an accident". But really, three times over 2 years? The third time, I went to the principal. It was a week before we were leaving on our winter vacation, and Mark needed those glasses. We had to pay more for a rush. She said that the boy who had broken them said it was an accident, he just wanted to try them on.....And he asked her to not tell his Dad, because his Dad would beat him. Then she said what floored me. "After all, you don't have to pay for them; it is just an inconvenience to you." I guess she was so used to everyone in that district being attached to a major car company somehow, and all things like glasses were paid for completely. I told her that no, we paid for these glasses ourselves and that they usually ran $250–300 dollars depending on if we needed new frames. I told her it had happened two times previously, same boy, always "an accident", if it ever happened again, I was calling the police and filing a report. I'm not sure what she told the kiddo, but he never broke a pair Mark's glasses again.

Mark

I did look into what the other kids were doing and tried to fit in. Maybe I tried too hard. What I do know that is living in Michigan, it's pretty cold through most of the year. I felt this made certain circumstances more difficult, like wearing cool clothes. Most cool shirts have short leaves and long sleeves look "dorky". It was sad but true, there is a code on being cool, and you have to dress a certain way. I tried to fit in, but I was always a wannabe. I tried everything to fit in, listened to the same music, and watched the same TV programs. But I never did fit in. I thought I was just a misanthrope.

In 7th grade, I stated going to a private school for children with learning disabilities. My parents thought I had a learning disability, but didn't know what it could be.

Mom

Mark did go to our local Middle School for 6th grade. And we did let the kiddos pick out their own clothes and shoes. The first day there, the same boy who broke glasses at elementary school smeared some sort of berry on Mark's shirt, basically ruining it. The counselor called me in and said that they were very aware of said kiddo, and that they would keep a close eye on him. He wasn't going to manipulate them like he had the people in elementary school. I was relieved. I don't remember much else unusual about that year, just that Mark kept up academically, didn't fit in but didn't seem too un-happy. We had already made the decision to move our OK to a private school. OK was just doing the very least to get by, we wanted OK on a college track. Mark too. We would have preferred Mark go to the same school as OK. There wasn't a spot in the elementary school, their elementary went through 6th grade We had him tested again in 7th grade. That school didn't think he could handle their academic curriculum, in reality; he would have worked hard and done fine academically, I'm not sure how he would have fit in socially. Most of the students at that school had been together since pre-K. As I've said, OK is a true extrovert. Socially fits right in anywhere. So, we looked into a local private LD school. Mark went there for 7th and 8th grade. It had small classes, 8 students and lots of support. I did like his 7th grade teacher a whole lot. She was strict, but fair. Mark studied hard, did really well academically, even played sports. I thought he was happy.

Mark

During that first year at the LD school, everything was going alright. I got to learn things I never knew before, like Greek Mythology. I liked how the Greeks explained everything in their myths, like why the sky doesn't fall down on us.

I do have to criticize about that school; they didn't allow sugar because "it caused hyperactivity" We all had to bring lunches from home because they didn't have a way to cook. Now, call me crazy, but I have a hard time reasoning with that. I do believe it is better for children to eat healthier. I have read that some researchers think sugar causing hyperactivity is a myth. That is not a statement that I can swear to, However, if sugar is so harmful, why isn't starch? This was during the early 1990's and in those days researchers were encouraging people to eat more starches, at least 6 a day. The thing is, starches are just longer strings of sugar, so if sugar is bad, starch must be worse.

Another thing I didn't like about the school was that every year, the school made all of us participate in a MANDITORY musical play. Every year, the school's division director put on a piece of garbage that was supposed to be fun. To me, that was just plain ludicrous. They made us dance choreographed pieces; there is no nice way of saying this, those productions just plain sucked. Doing dorky gestures and reciting lame scripts isn't fun when you are forced to do it. And to this day, I don't know what the director meant by continually saying that this was "our" play. This made me want to ask "what the f**k are you talking about"? We had to do your lame-ass play with your lame-ass songs, everything choreographed your way. That is just my point of view. I wonder if I would have felt better if she would have admitted that it was her play done her way and really not our play at all. Most of the children did not have fun doing this play. We were all miserable together. I wonder if it was even legal, making us participates in something we hated? I don't think it would be in a public school, but this was a private one. Maybe the ACLU could have found a loophole so we wouldn't have had to be in the play if we didn't want to. I'm not saying that I support the ACLU, but maybe here they could have helped us. The second year there was barely any academics and I was bored.

Mom

I thought those plays were pretty lame too; I never knew he hated them. I thought he was happy at that school. He did well academically, made friends, played basketball, got contacts and got his braces off. Mark was one nice looking teenager. I've said I liked his 7th grade teacher. His 8th grade teacher was good but a bit of a push over. She was a tiny thing and had all boys in her class, 8 of them. . I had a premonition that there might be problems at the first parents' meeting. She said the one thing she didn't allow was being silly. She would put anyone's name on the board that was silly. And, if the boys saw her being silly, they could put her name on the board. It wasn't a bad year, looking back though; the boys were in charge most of the time. We decided that we would look at other schools for HS for Mark, even though this school went through the 12th grade.

Mark

I don't hate acting. In fact, I went to Theater Camp for two summers. We were outside a lot. The first play we did was called Confessions. I played a character called Frank that was a jealous husband. A cute blond girl played his clever, pranky wife called Maude. She was making her husband, me, jealous by telling about the first man she flirted with, she went on and on about it. In the end, she reveals that she was only 3 years old at the time. Our play was on a Sunday, a lot of people came to see it and we got a standing ovation.

I also like telling jokes. Some people have said that I am funny. I've tried to use some wit writing this memoir. I have kind of lost touch with acting, but I still like telling jokes. I guess humor has always been a part of me. Most people, except my OS, told me I was good at acting. Maybe OS was just jealous.

I am good at acting if I like the script and have some say in the production. That's why the plays weren't fun at the LD school. I thought that maybe I should go to Hollywood and become rich. I was aware that fame has its price, there will be people out there who just hate you and degrade you and believe crazy rumors about you! I also realize only a tiny number of people who try for the Hollywood spot light get it. It wouldn't be special if everyone made it big. Let's just say that I did beat the odds and achieved fame, would I last? My career could go down the tubes in 2-3 years. I know now that Hollywood doesn't like conservatives or religious people. That fact alone guarantees I wouldn't go far. I would like to do plays and things on the local level, with likeminded people. Do I think I'm the best in the world? No, but I'm pretty darned good.

Mom

Hum....I remember Theater Camp and the cute plays, scenes that they did. Mark did a great job in everything he was in, we enjoyed watching him perform. I would never have thought that humor was a part of him. Mark did and still does take most things literally. Very literally. I remember in 6th grade, him reading me a chapter in The Red Badge of Courage. He read a passage about the serpentine line of men going up the mountain. I stopped him and asked what that meant to him. He said that there was a snake on the trail and the soldiers were stepping over it. I don't know if this is part of being AS or not. He does not appreciate being the butt of a joke. I think whenever he gets the employment thing under control, he should see if there is still such a thing as Little Theater. Mark is great at memorizing lines, inflections and all. It would be a fun outlet for him. I'm not sure his wife would enjoy being on stage but there are lots of other things one can do to help out on a production.

Mark, High School Years

I chose a Lutheran school for high school, it wasn't far from home. This gave me a lot of my spiritual insight. I am definitely a conservative Christian. At the time, I was an Episcopal, like my family, and I felt the Episcopal Church suited my beliefs. The LHS brought Christianity into my life every school day. There is much about the Lutherans I admire, and I am grateful that I went to that school. I do believe that they brought good into my life. Those teachers do a whole lot for very little money. They had positions of authority but they knew they weren't exempt from social rules and would admit when they were wrong. They gave me a more detailed outlook on the bible than my church did; I felt that I was growing closer to God. These people were serious about a good education, and I do believe that I did receive a good education from them. They were also concerned with the moral conditions of this crazy world. I feel that they stood by their integrity and gave good moral guidance. I believe that they taught me a lot of good information about God.

There are things I would criticize about my HS. They are theologically more conservative than even the Episcopal Church. They do take the bible very literally, I'm not sure this is always a good thing. I have a hard time understanding their attitude towards Darwinism theory of evolution. Now, I'm not saying that one needs to accept that whole theory. Or that you have to accept the theory of creationism. I have found holes in both theories. And, it seems that a true Christian is only concerned about where he is heading, not what he came from. I think that there are more concerning things going on in today's world. Colleges and universities are teaching revisionist history. The media helps them with these revisions. Now there are people who disrespect everything the US stands for and are willing to kill us for our beliefs! There seem to be whole societies that have forsaken God. There are many more dire issues now than whether or not evolution is taught.

Another thing I have a bit of a problem with is the Lutherans' attitude towards Mormons. The Mormons had some unusual beliefs, and had practiced polygamy. Mormons I have met say that they don't believe in more than one wife anymore. Mormons are more respectful and Christian sect that either the Lutheran or the Episcopal. I do agree that we need better race relations. I also think its crap that Episcopalians tell me that President Bush was evil, and I must accept homosexuality as being morally right. They also say that capitalism is bad, but they seem to have lots of money. Hypocrites. I lost faith in my Episcopal church, and did leave it though it took many years for me to leave.

I do have a few bad memories. I choked a girl. Not hard, but I reacted without thinking. She had a locker closed to mine and liked to tease me. She even teased me a lot in English class. I tried to keep my cool, but one day she slapped at my eye and I lost it, grabbed her shoulders by her neck and shook her. I stopped immediately. We both had to see the councilor and I regretted it. I got one day in school suspension and I had to help in the cafeteria. It actually felt good, like I was making amends.

My football team had team dinners Friday nights before our Saturday game. They used to ask me if I would do impressions, or tell jokes. I never knew if they were laughing with me or at me. One time I thought they were trying to humiliate me. I grabbed a pizza and ran.

I was also never good at talking about sex. I remember saying that I liked girls, not guys. I'm not gay; I just don't like talking about sex. I know now that it is one of my autistic sensitive spots.

I didn't get a date to homecoming junior. year, but I did go with a group of both girls and guys. Senior year I thought I couldn't get a date either. My mom and dad said that there was a girl that liked me; they heard that from another football parent. She was a cheerleader, and a junior. My parents wanted me to ask her. I was a little afraid. They said that as a backup plan, they had a young friend from my dad's office that would go with me. I asked the girl from HS, she said yes. We went all out, tux, flowers, limo, dinner. It was good. Dad had had another promotion, and we were moving to Dallas after the prom and graduation. I did go back the next fall and took her to homecoming, at my old HS.

Another bad memory came from my job. I was a bagger at a local grocery store. The guys from my football team asked me if I ever bagged Maxi pads. I said no, just douches…they didn't know what that was. I said it's for cleaning, and I couldn't get the words out. I really don't like to talk about these matters.

My Jr year, we took a driving Spring Break vacation to DC. We played tourist and saw things that I hadn't seen since I was in elementary school and we lived in suburban Virginia. Then we drove up to NY to see my OS at college.

Mom

I have to break in here. This was the spring that there was that awful bombing in Oklahoma City. We were in DC, staying right across the street from the White House. Everything shut down. There were men with things in their ears all over the place to include our hotel lobby. It was scary. Strange that Mark doesn't even mention it.

Mark

Another memory is my 17th birthday. We had a pool, so I invited some friends over for a pool party. I didn't tell them it was my birthday. I helped get things ready, cleaned my room, cleaned our our rec room, even put balloons on my mail box in our school colors. 4 people showed up. I was really depressed. My OS knew how badly I felt so we went to see some of OS's friends that were home from college for the summer. We drove around and smoked weed. It was my first time; I got buzzed and liked how that felt. I smoked more weed with OS that summer, I was even paid in weed to clean OS's cat's litter box. OS brought home a stray that was sick and couldn't mix with our other cats. We even smoked pot and went to a Grateful Dead concert. I was worried the security people would know, it made me paranoid. We did go into the concert and did have a great time. I even danced and made a fool of myself, buy hey, it was a Dead concert. My OS can be fun and nice at times, but I think really likes to get me worked up. And OS is lazy, and loves arguing with people just for the sake of arguing. I think OS has Narcissi Personality Disorder. I didn't want to be like that, so I never smoked pot again.

Mom

I had NO idea about the pot. I did know that the kiddos snuck beer occasionally, and I did know that OK had a friend with all sorts of problems, like marijuana use, stealing etc. That friend went to another school so they didn't see each other daily. Big problem for us was that

that kiddo's parents were old friends of ours; they did know of their kiddo's problems and were trying to deal with them. These old friends of ours that just happened to end up in the Detroit area the same time we did. They thought that our OK was a good influence on their kiddo. Guess we were all wrong.

Mark

I visited my OS College again, this time by myself. I flew up. I met my OS's roommate, we played some cards, and I got drunk for the first time at a college party. I drank beer and smoked. My OS saw me, and wanted me to go back to our room. I just wanted to lie down. One friend of OK's friends came to talk to me. I'm told that I babbled on and on. OS babbled when drunk too, guess it runs in the family. This was my first taste of college life.

Mom

We were glad when Mark chose to go to a Lutheran HS. It had a good reputation, good graduation record and a high number of their grads went on to college. Another plus was it wasn't too far from our home. We met with his counselor before school started. She took one look at Mark and said he was a big kid, how about being on the football team? Mark played varsity football all 4 years. He was also on the wrestling team and the track team. He lettered in two of the sports and got a letterman's jacket. He did really well academically. He seemed to have friends, and a social life. I thought that he was happy and accepted. He did go to Homecoming every year, with a group usually. And he had his own car from January of his junior year. I thought that was pretty special.

We, the parents did plan the first all-night party for the graduates. I had helped OK's party, so wanted to be a part of this too. And we chaperoned even though the movers were coming that next day to start packing us up for our move to Texas. I was tired beyond belief, but I was really excited about the new home. We used an architect and built our dream retirement home. What Mark doesn't say is that I stayed in Michigan so he could finish his last two years of HS. Dad had accepted a new position two years earlier with his company in Dallas. He flew home weekends; I stayed so Mark could graduate with his class. It was an awful time for me, I really didn't like the weather in Michigan, and I absolutely love Dallas. We were able to plan and have a great home built that two years, Dad brought home pictures weekly with the progress being made on the new house. I did have the responsibility of keeping everything going at the Michigan home, get it ready to sell, figure out what we were taking and what we were leaving, and volunteering at our church. I was kept busy during the very last winter we spent in Michigan that gave us another Mark-ism. It's December 21, the house was decorated, cards done, presents bought, wrapped, shipped, let the celebrations begin. Dad and OK are home for the holiday, it should have been a great time. I love holidays as much as Mark does, all our traditions, but I always got depressed after Christmas. I always felt that after Christmas, we had a long, hard, dark, cold, slog until the spring. Mark looked at the calendar and said "Look Mom, we are going on the downhill side of dark"! That was referring to the fact that the days were now supposed to be getting longer....hard to tell in Michigan, it was dark at 5 pm and not light until almost 9 in the AM. I'm really affected by light, so winters in Michigan were really hard for me. I was touched that Mark had noticed and was trying to cheer me up.

Mark

Back to my HS years. I played sports all four of my years, football, baseball, wrestling. Going to a small private school makes it easy to be part of a team. I had to learn everything, we had a galloping movement we had to do in Football, and I thought it made me look like a horse, so my nickname became Horse. During practice, I would often stare out at the road. Speed fascinated me, not sure why. During football season, the parents host a dinner the Friday before our Saturday game. We went to a team member's home and the parents did the meal. I hosted all 4 years; my Mom ordered lots of pizza for dinner and had raw veggies as a salad, and soda. Another mother would bring the desserts. I felt I had egg on my face because my Mom didn't make something like the other mothers did, but it turned out to be a really big hit. The team looked forward to our dinner each season. We played Saturday afternoon games. And we practiced every day; sometimes I felt like football took over my life, eat, sleep, school, and practice. And I even managed to work a few hours at the local grocery store. Because we went to church on Sundays, I had no time to sleep in I'm not a morning person, so this was hard. And I don't like being out in the cold and Michigan is cold for most of football season. I stuck with it and played football for all 4 years. It was easier after the first year, I think having to plan on practice and games made me do better in school. My school wasn't known for winning, but I got my picture in the local paper making a really great tackle. I got the team Captain Crunch award that week.

On New Year's Eve when I was a Jr, I was home alone with my OS. I noticed my new Rolling Stones CD was scratched. I yelled about borrowing my things and ruining them. OS got mad and wouldn't speak to me. Our parents had left us some Champaign to have at midnight. I drank the whole bottle, and then wanted more. I took three beers and drank them. I was really drunk, and ended up getting sick. OS was leaving for college the next day, I didn't care. OS had been a jerk the whole vacation. I took an aspirin before going sleep and woke up without a hangover. I ended up helping Mom and Dad start undecorating.

I played baseball my sophomore year. I wasn't very good at it, coach suggested I try track. I did track for 2 years, even won a few races. It was a good experience for me.

Spring of 1997. I took up cigars. I didn't inhale, just liked how it looked. My parents were cool about it; I guess they thought I would get tired of it. They did make my clothes smell. Cigars were becoming an in thing to do; it was sort fun even thought I knew it wasn't really good for you. It can cause oral cancer.

I met a nice girl my senior year. My Spanish teacher introduced us. She was a Jr and a cheerleader. I took her to Homecoming that year, and to prom. We were both really socially backward, really quiet, didn't know how to talk to another. Maybe she had some form of Autism too.

She was pretty, but I don't think she was as good a student as I was. I actually flew to Detroit to take her to homecoming her senior year.

I had a tutor during my study hall to help me. I did even better academically my Sr year without a tutor.

I went to visit my OS again my senior year. OS kissed me in front a bunch of people, I really hated that.

So, in summing up my HS years, I made some good friends, did pretty good academically. Because I went to a small private school, I was able to play on any team I wanted. That was nice; I played football the whole 4 years.

I did suffer from anxiety and depression I think the depression was made worst by the weather, winters in MI. We had very little sun, I get very down and sad, I know now that this is an actual disorder. I love living where there is lots of sun. My senior year, I did get closer to my peers. I was sad we were leaving for Dallas area, but was happy about the new custom home that was 1.5 times bigger than the old one, and since it was custom built, we got exactly what we wanted. So, it was hard to leave the friends I had just managed to make, but nice to go to a warmer sunnier place and a new home.

Mom

Once again, I am floored. I thought Mark was happy and adjusted well to HS. He was a big, good looking kiddo with a killer smile. He did well in his classes because he worked and studied hard. He played lots of sports, went to the dances, and had his own car for his last two years. He had a part time job from the time he was 15. We knew the move to Dallas area would be hard for him. We also knew from our OK, that HS friendships fade bit even when your family stays in the same place. People went off to college and formed new friendships. Now with email, it's a bit easier to keep up with that mobile population. The move was a bit hard for our OK too. OK had basically been away for 3 years, but considered Michigan home. OK was home that first summer in the new Texas home, stating over too. OK was rough on Mark that summer, teasing him arguing with him for no good reason, just making all our lives a bit rocky. I was personally so wrapped up in the beautiful new home, that I just ignored the snarking. I think we were all a bit relieved when OK went back for the final year of college way up in New York.

Mark, Dallas area and my college years

I got a job working in a local grocery store, started as a bagger. I wanted to move up so asked for a cashiering position. I blew the first try at cashiering. I don't like to fail, so tried gain and passed the test. I got lots of customer compliments, even though I thought that one of the supervisors didn't like me. Remember, I hadn't been identified as AS and wouldn't be for several years. I did come across as weird at times. I also started at the local community college and took a class that summer. I did a pretty good job of balancing class and job and getting settled in a new place. I did get lost coming home after a study session. I knew that there was a big water tower by our new sub, so, when I made a wrong turn and realized I had gotten on the wrong road, I started looking for a water tower and went toward it. I got even more lost. What I didn't know or realize yet was that there are water towers all over the Dallas area. Luckily, I did have a cell phone and called home. This is before we all had GPS systems, and cell phones didn't have them either. When I called home, Mom told me that there are lots of water towers in Dallas. She had a great map, so she talked me to the right roads to get home. That was scary. I was able to move to another community college campus that was closer to our home.

My OS was a real jerk that summer home, barging in my room, locked the bathroom door from the other side, our bedrooms each had our own sink and toilet, we shared a shower that was in the middle. OS argued with me, knew I had a problem with gay rights, so brought that up a whole lot. I don't hate gay people, I just don't condone gayness. OS also argued with me about my Christianity. Anyway, OS went back to college in NY and my life got easier. I met a new girl, I met her friends, I liked them but I got the feeling that they didn't like me. Anyway, life was good while it lasted. We only lived there for two years, and then we moved again. Dad retired, but was offered a new opportunity that he said was just too good and too much fun to pass up. I was able to finish

2 years of Community College, and I did have my own apartment for the last year. So, I worked, went to school, lived on my own, dated, really handled things pretty darned good, I think. Then comes another move, or stay in Texas on my own at one of the universities Dad and I looked at. Dad also took me to look at schools in North Carolina, where my parents would be moving.

So, only two years and we were going to North Carolina. Dad took me on a college tour of 4 schools in NC, I had applied to and been accepted at in North Carolina. I decided on a small Baptist college. because I could get a private room. My mother thought that I would do better with a private room than a shared one. My OS lived in a co-op at college, almost a commune... I think she was wrong, and I could have gotten along sharing a room with someone who respected my things.

Mom

In a perfect world, Mark would have had a roommate who respected his things. That rarely happens in my limited experience. He was better off not sharing a room. That move was hard for 3 of us. I loved the Dallas house, but hadn't made friends yet either, just company ones. I also knew that if Dad didn't try this new opportunity to help a promising start up go public, he would always wonder. So we moved to the Triangle Area, North Carolina

Mark

At first, I thought that my small Baptist College would really work out for me. I had attended Lutheran HS, so knew how strict religious schools could be. I started to have what I now know are anxiety attacks. Everyone seemed to know each other, they went to church together. It's a Baptist school; most of the students went to the campus church. They were mainly from the Triangle area. I unfortunately got a suite with members of the wrestling team; they asked me to move to another dorm so they could all be together. I did. I didn't realize how different it was going to be going to a small college in a small town out in the country

I have always lived in cities. And, there were lots of tests. I'm not good at taking tests; I tense up and forget things I know. I was really having a hard time, but I really didn't want to fail. I asked about tutoring, but was told to wait a few weeks. Not a good idea for me as it made me more anxious. I was having trouble fitting in; I had trouble keeping my dorm room in shape where I could find things. I really like to watch WWE. I found some other fans, but they liked the Rock while I liked Mick Foley. That took a lot of fun out of watching the Monday night program. I had some friends, both boys and girls, on the soccer team, so I would go watch them play. I really don't care much for soccer, but it was something to do. I prefer football, but my new college didn't have a team. I played all sorts of sports in HS because it was a small school and everyone who wanted to play was on the team. It doesn't work that way in college.

I did go to a Methodist church in the nearby town. I enjoyed the sermons, and the bible study. The pastor was nice too. They were more fundamental than I was used to, but ok. As I've said new college is Baptist. Most of the students are too.

I actually made it through that first year, but barely. I started drinking heavily. It is a dry campus and you couldn't drink in your room, so I would drink at off campus parties. I thought that this was an ok thing to do. I thought I was pretty popular because I was invited to off campus parties by some really cute girls. I later figured it out that they liked me because I had a car and a credit card and was old enough to by the booze. They even told me it was ok to drink in their off campus house. Later found out that no student is supposed to drink anywhere on campus, in the town, in their own rented house, etc.

Anyway, my drinking got really bad. I would drink enough to get high really fast. I never drove while I was drinking which is good thing. I did black out several times and a friend got me back to the dorm. I opted to stay on campus for the first summer session so I could get a few more classes I needed to transfer to large local university out of the way. I had decided by then that this college wasn't for me. I got into real trouble over the Memorial Day holiday. There was another party at the cute girls' house. We were discussing Dawson's Creek, the TV show, for some reason. I got really drunk and lost all my inhibitions, I guess I got so obnoxious that they told me to leave. I started back to the dorm, and then decided to go back to the party. They locked me out; I banged so hard on the door that I broke the glass and cut my hand. I couldn't drive, and felt so badly about breaking the glass that I called the police on myself. They were nice and took me to the nearest hospital where I needed stiches. They also called my parents. That was the worst night of my life. My parents came to take me back home for the rest of the weekend. When I went back to class, I still felt so badly that I went to the head of the college and told him what I had done. He told me then that no student is to drink anywhere while they are a student. I told him that there were off campus parties, and I thought that the girls would be turning themselves in too. I didn't tell him their names. Well, they never did. I decided to leave and not finish that summer class, just go back home and concentrate on getting accepted to large local university.

Mom

Another eye opener. We knew that Mark was unhappy at his new college, but had no idea he was drinking, or that he was financing the parties. Yes, the cute girls lied to him. Big surprise, kiddo with a car and a credit card and of age, they would go with him to another town a few towns away from college and tell him what to buy. He was invited to their parties as payback I guess. I should have noticed the credit card bills, I didn't. Maybe they said some other kind of store? Or he got cash, using his card? I was pretty wrapped up on being an empty nester and getting settled in the new community. Husband was brought in to be a big wig, so we had lots of invitations places, and I was working with an architect to build another perfect home, this one on a hillside. Life was good except for the fact that I had become obese. I found a bariatric surgeon who just happened to be here in the area who had a new minimally invasive surgery for weight loss. I looked into it; it was a several month process as the Dr. didn't want you to have unrealistic expectations. I had the surgery and lost the weight. 19 years later, it's still off though I now have to watch what I eat, like a normal person.

Mark Thompson

Mark

So, I moved to back to our home in the Triangle Area, but couldn't get into large local university until I made up the few classes I was short. I took them at a couple of places; the Baptist College had satellite campus in Raleigh, and another community college. It took another year, and then I was accepted to large local university. I got a job cashiering at a local grocery chain. They had a store fairly close to campus. I had asked to take tests in a noise free room, but had to be evaluated, The Neuropsychiatric department of large local university hospital confirmed that I was indeed Asperger's. Finally, a diagnosis after all these years.

I entered large local university and got involved with an adult autistic social group. I made a few good friends, one was another fan of the WWE, and we liked to talk politics. The other was a bit older than the rest of us. He was also a WWE fan. I saw him a lot at the grocery store because it was by his apartment and he couldn't drive. . Anyway, this social group was for adults like me who are autistic. We went out to dinner, saw movies, got together and just had fun. There were usually 10-15 of us, mostly guys, who would come to these meetings. The group got smaller and smaller and after a few years, the group was disbanded due to lack of interest and to budget cuts. That was very depressing because I lost a social group who accepted me for what I was, and understood how difficult it is to be autistic in today's world.

I worked at the grocery store my whole time at large local university. It was a job that would work around my hours at school, and gave me a bit of extra money. I had moved back home because my parents lived 10 minutes away from campus. People aren't always nice to cashiers, they complain about prices, talk politics, and get mad when you ask for ID for alcohol or tobacco. I didn't make the rules, but I did have to follow them I did manage to get the respect of my employers, and that made me feel good.

The diagnosis of AS did make my life a bit easier because it gave my problem a name. For too many of my childhood years my family and I wrestled with shadows. I had to enter large local university as a non degree seeking student until I made up those few classes. I had all the math and science credits I needed to get into a Michigan university, and small Baptist College, but not enough for large local university. And I couldn't make them up at large local university, so that's why I ended up taking classes at different campuses, I was able to get a statistics class and a trig class, got B's and was eventually accepted to the status of degree seeking student.

I also joined a Methodist youth group spring of 2001. I was ready to leave the Episcopal Church for good. I really liked the Methodist group. It was a lot of fun; I met a girl named X. and became infatuated with her. She was very liberal, but we could have good conversions. We often went out for coffee or lunch but really weren't boyfriend-girlfriend. I eventually told her I was autistic, and she was shocked. She respected my intelligence and thought that I took a lot of time to think out a problem. She was kind and gentle. She was pretty, had lots of friends, made good grades, but got very depressed at times. Just after spring semester started, I got the awful news via the youth group listseve that she had committed suicide. That was the saddest day of my life so far. I went to campus, and it hurt me to see everyone going on like nothing happened. One of our own classmates was so depressed that she took her own life. I wanted to yell at them. A wonderful, kind, bright girl had just ended her life, how could things continue on so normally. I slowly left the group, I didn't think that they took her taking her life seriously enough. I guess all groups are the same, they pretend to be one thing, open and loving, but then can't accept that someone can be different and still good. I did go to two memorial services for her. I certainly hope she didn't go to hell. She was really a good person even if her politics were a whole lot more liberal than mine. I respected her, she was bight and smart and kind. I never really felt a part of the youth group after that; they seemed to forget about her because she did something not condoned by the church.

Mom

I knew that the young woman had taken her own life. I didn't know Mark took is so personally. I guess they got along because they were both a bit different, and then she was gone. Over the years, I've come up with a visual for how our AS person handled emotional upset. I compare it to a pebble being tossed in a pond, the first ring out is how does this affect me. The next ring is how it will affect others around me; next ring is how I can help. Mark gets stuck in the first ring, how this will affect me and my life. It's not that he is uncaring; he just needs help in seeing that this isn't all about him, and how to react with compassion. I guess the irony is that he does feel very deeply for others, just doesn't know how to show it or express it verbally.

Mark

After that, felt totally different about that youth group. They were really just as closed minded as a lot of Christian sects. You had to agree with them, or you weren't a good person. They even had a minister who thought it was awful to have corporate affiliations, who thought that God was mad at America for waging wars, but thought it was ok to be an atheist. She also thought it was ok to be homosexual. I don't think I can condone it, but I wouldn't hold it against a person. I do believe that marriage is sacred and is just between and man and a woman. This woman claimed to appreciate all sides, but only was interested in pushing her own agenda. I also don't feel it's appropriate to compare being gay with being black.

I also had some problems with the university seeming to teach that it wrong for a conservative group to speak on campus, but it's ok for a liberal group speaks on questionable things. The very liberal groups say that they love and include everyone. But that's only every one who thinks and acts like them. I thought it was the purpose of a university to expose the student to different views, to earn to question and to learn to think. I feel this has been lost

I did graduate from large local university in 2004. I got a degree in Sociology, with 3 plus grade average. I graduated mid-year, and yes, it did take me a while. I was in three colleges, universities and three moves. I invited a lady who help me, tutored me, in subjects I found confusing. We all went out to dinner afterwards. My Dad had been in NYC during 9-11. He told us exactly what it was like to be there during that time. I should have been more worried.

Unfortunately, graduating from college doesn't always mean a job. I kept my cashiering job while looking. I don't look for jobs well, I find it like looking for a needle in a haystack. I thought that the autism people or VR might be of help. They tried, but really haven't been able to do much.

Mom

I have to interrupt here. It never occurred to us that Mark wasn't using all the campus help to get position after graduating. Apparently his advisor never told him to check the career center, neither did we. Things that we take for granted often go right by him. VR people were of minimal help. In fairness to them, they have huge workloads and Mark wasn't in any crisis like no housing or destitute, so he wouldn't have been high priority. They also seem to assume that all AS people can only work limited hours and have get Disability. Mark doesn't get any government help, then or now, and needs the hours and benefits full time employment offers. They did find part time jobs for him, but nothing that could turn into a career. One well-meaning person suggested he volunteer to get a job....so Mark volunteered for a year at another big Triangle Area University. He worked transcribing for a grad student. It went well, she finished her project, and he of course, didn't get a job interview. I am also surprised that having his Dad up in NYC during 9-11 didn't make more of an impression. I was mentally struggling with the fact that the startup Dad came to North Carolina to help grow went bankrupt. We didn't start our second dream home, but did buy a nice big home. Dad quickly found another opportunity, up in NYC. I didn't want to move there, he thought it would be fairly short term, so he rented an apartment. It was just off Wall Street, walking distance from the Towers. Mark and I had visited there the previous summer. Little did we know that Dad would be there for such a tragedy, I'm surprised it hasn't affected him more. That business closed and Dad came home for good.

Mark

At times, I felt that VR didn't understand me. I was able to get a part time job with another large Triangle Area university library. I really liked it. Unfortunately, they gave the permanent job to another person. I was crushed. My Mom suggested going back to school to get another skill. She suggested bookkeeping. So, I went to a local Community college for an AA in bookkeeping. I did really well. I was asked to join the Theta Phi Betta Honor society. At about this time, I decided to try networking with the Jaycees. They were in Raleigh. I did enjoy them, but wasn't able to be as active as I would like because of studying, so I dropped out. I also continued to cashier, now I really didn't like it but thought that having the degree in Accounting would help. I did get the degree, but it didn't help much in getting a real career.

Mom

I did suggest accounting to Mark because a friend who was a retired CPA convinced me it would be a good match. It could have been. Accounting now is really bookkeeping, and anyone can buy a computer program to do it. Intellectually, I do think Mark could have become a CPA, but realistically no. There are things that are legally allowed, but maybe not moral right. Mark couldn't handle that at all, and wouldn't be very diplomatic. I feel badly about aiming him in that direction. And, once again, we never thought to tell him to use campus services in job placement, and his advisor didn't either.

I have to add here that Mark is very moral; there are few shades of gray in his world. Things are right or wrong. Rules are to be followed. Speed limits to be observed. I'm not sure if this is true of all AS people, but it certainly is of our Mark.

Mark

While I was at local Community College, Dad lost his part time consulting job. He was on a business trip to New Zealand when the company called him to say that they had decided on going another direction, and he wasn't needed anymore. I was having trouble in a class, but I felt that I couldn't stress my parents out even though I was having trouble. And to make it worse, it was just before Christmas.

Mom

Again, interesting interpretation of Dad's job loss. This job was to be a fun, 3rd career. It was an annoyance, but not a disaster. Dad has a retirement from his first company; we had saved and invested so there really wasn't a problem. I thought that it could be a learning experience for Mark. People who are really good at their jobs can lose them for no good reason. Guess he didn't see this, and projected it on himself.

After told me he had to drop a class, I had a real revelation about the ability of our young people to think and reason. Mark asked to get a tutor to help with a difficult part of a class. The professor said he had to teach something called Peachtree even though no one used it any more, it was difficult, but they had to learn it. That's all Mark needed to hear. So, he found a very pleasant young man to help with the Peachtree part. Peachtree came with a computer download that you needed to do the homework and pass that part of the class. Problem, it was for PCs and Mark had a Mac. They called the textbook distributer to see if a Mac version was available. No. So what could they do? They came up with the idea to use a computer in the CC's computer lab that had Peachtree loaded. Ok. They reserved time on that computer. That might have worked except for the fact that it often was down, or someone else was on it and asked for just a bit more time…..well Mark got so far behind that he had to drop the whole class. I was confused. He had a tutor. I sat him down and we walked through what I thought were obvious steps. Did you try and see if they made it in Mac version. Yes, they don't. Ok, there are 3 PCs at home. Did you ever think of asking to borrow one for this section of the class? No. Did you talk to Apple? No. I had a vague memory of a program that could be installed that would allow a machine to run PC to Mac programs and vice versa. I talked to the nice men at the Apple store. Yes, buy it and have it installed, then you can run either version. In a few hours, I had thought out the problem, and found several solutions. We bought the program, had it installed so the next time Mark took that class, he could do the homework at his own speed. Honestly, what are the Universities teaching these days?

Mark

I did eventually get through all the cases and did graduate with honors. That was really a positive thing. But getting a job in Accounting isn't as easy as I thought it would be. So, I'm still cashiering at the grocery store. I asked to have a different position a few times, but was never given one. Now I'm feeling like a total failure. Two college degrees and a dead end job. I really don't want to make a pile of money, but I do want and crave prestige.

Mom

I would like to know where this need/want for prestige comes from. His one awful teacher? He has achieved a whole lot, but he can't see it. He constantly compares himself with OK. OK has two degrees too, and isn't using either. OK has followed a hobby and is one of the managers at their specialty store... I've tried to explain to Mark that being a manager means OK opens up, closes up, mops floors, and cleans the bathrooms, deals with clientele and so on. Makes no difference, OK has the title of manager.

Mark

I met my future wife, Claire in 2008. I had started a Myspace page in an attempt to make friends and maybe get some job contacts. Claire responded to my profile because I graduated from the same college that she had graduated from. First we communicated via e-mail, then by phone, and then we met for the first time at a Barnes and Noble. It was a nice, neutral place to sit and talk. I felt an immediate attraction for her, we talked and talked. I walked her to her car, and gave her a kiss on the cheek. I went home feeling really good. That was early October. We saw each other for 4-6 weeks and decided that we really were compatible and it was safe to say we had become a couple. We both like coffee shops, Kings Dominion and the beach. We are both very conservative and very Christian. I was now a Methodist, she a Baptist. We are really good for each other; we boost each other up when we are down.

Mom

I think that Claire is the best thing that has ever happened to Mark. She is a truly a nice, sweet person. Maybe a bit too nice at times. When Mark first told me he had met someone over the internet, I was concerned. We have a nice address, Mark drove a fairly new Acura, and he was a grad of our local university. I was afraid that he is a bit naïve at times and might be taken advantage of. Mark told me that Claire and her Mom wanted to meet both of us....ok. We arranged to meet at Cheesecake Factory and had a lovely afternoon. Both Claire and her Mom came across as warm, caring people. This was apparent from the first meeting. I was thinking the day over when I got home, and came to the conclusion that her Mom was checking us out! Claire is such a caring person, that she tends to see only the good in a person, her Mom was making sure she wasn't going to be taken advantage of by Mark. I'm sure both of us Moms had a good feeling about the other's child.

Claire

Where to begin? Mark, how I met him. I was upstairs working on my computer and decided to give "My Space" a shot. The picture of Mark was cute, and I saw local University's l wallpaper on his page. So, I said, Ok, maybe this guy is a keeper. He had a long description of all the places he had traveled to, and I remember how much he liked Rome. Finally, he answered me, and we started talking on the phone.

One night I was talking with him, and I asked him why he had an Autism logo on his page. He said he has Asperger's. At first, I was sad about that, but I kept talking with him and the more we talked the more we had in common. I thought to myself, everyone has an Achilles heel, so what would be wrong with meeting this guy? Turns out, nothing! We met at Barnes & Noble. I knew who to look for because I had seen his picture and he looked great! I remember he had a backpack full of books and was sitting in the coffee section. We met and the rest is history. For 10 years, we drove back and forth to each other's homes. We lived in opposite ends of the Triangle. We dated 10 years before we got married. His parents are the sweetest couple in the world, and I am glad to be a part of their family.

Mark is the smartest guy I have ever met. He loves talking about history and sports. When he talks about history, I mainly listen or ask questions because he is so brilliant. When we talk about sports, we focus on similar players who we enjoy watching, especially large local university team players and coaches.

Because of Mark, I have a deeper love of the Carolina Panthers. We drove together to see them in Charlotte a few times and it was a blast! Mark is a good driver although he has issues with depth perception. He always tells me that it's easier for him to make right turns than left, and he has a hard time going in reverse, especially parking! He does wear contacts, but sometimes I worry about him. That's just life. I know he worries about me too, but it's okay now because we are together.

A long time ago I thought I would become a successful writer. Turns out, that's kind of a joke. But here I am writing again, so maybe, this night before his birthday, I will be able to portray what it's like living with someone with Asperger's. Some people may not know what this is. I will tell you: it is not easy. Mark will tell you, living with Aspergers is like wrestling with demons. Maybe that is one reason he watches so much WWE. It has gotten to the point where I watch it with him every now and then. I don't mind because I love him so much. If watching WWE makes him happy so be it!

There has been a lot in the news about Asperger's. It is a higher functioning form of autism. Now some people with autism are much lower functioning than Mark. In fact, a lot of people are. But not Mark. He can do so much! I am glad he is willing and able to work. However, right now, he is not happy. His mom wants him to get a new job, and I agree. He would be much happier working somewhere else. The reason being is that the hours he works now are not orthodox. He needs something more stable...it would help me out too! But this is not about me. It is about him. I love him so much that I want him to find what he is looking for. And right now, that is a new job.

Mark claims that he has been misguided. He tells me that some people over the years have told him he would not become successful and that is a shame. Yes. A shame. I have tried to help him find what he is looking for, but only God knows where it is. He keeps applying for jobs, but it seems like no one will accept him. I have told him a higher power is looking out for him, and I truly believe Christ is. The whole Asperger's thing is what hinders him. If he had different social skills, another company may be willing to hire him.

He gets anxious during interviews and while taking tests. At times, he is a slow reader, but if people could see what I see in him, they would know he is an Ace!

When we first started talking, Mark wrote a blog. Mostly about his opinions of the day. Sometimes about what he had done. To my knowledge he does not blog anymore. He told me today he would like a hobby. Maybe I could tell him to blog again! Once this is finished, if all goes well, he probably will!

Also, I have tried to tell him not to be too angry about his past, and I am hoping he will soon find a way to forgive certain people.

Mark, if you are reading this, you can do it! When you trust in God, you can do anything!

Paul once said, "I can do all things through Christ which strengthened me." -Philippians 4:13

Someone even greater than Paul, Jesus, once said, 'I am the vine, ye are the branches: He that abideth in me, and I in him, the same bringeth forth much fruit: for without me ye can do nothing• -John 5:15

Mark

Ok, I had two degrees and still not a great job. I'm not terrible computer literate, and didn't feel I could ask my family for more help.

My OS married, that made me feel a bit happier. I like the spouse, all 4 of us get along, but aren't best friends.

Mom

About this time, I started to realize that we weren't a big part of Mark's life anymore. That's a bit sad for any parent. He moved home, but we rarely saw him. He stayed busy with Claire and job hunting, and keeping his cashiering job. I knew he wasn't happy with the cashiering, and bookkeeping didn't seem to be going anywhere. I listen to a lot of radio, and eventually bought into the commercials for a very for profit IT school. They promise you can have a great IT job in months even with no computer experience. Well, this sounded perfect for Mark. He's not computer savvy, neither are we. He is very intelligent, and wouldn't be working with people. We went with him to interview them while they were interviewing him. We made them aware of his autism, not a problem for them. Mark was given a test to see if he was compatible and able to do the work. Guess what? He was.

It was $23,000 to take the course, and he could actually take it in their building, not on line. We paid for the class as it seemed like this might be the answer to his employment problems. Mark attended all the classes did all the homework, passed the tests with flying colors. What he couldn't do was pass the certification test and without that he wasn't going to get a job. There were even practice certification tests, but they didn't help. It never occurred to us that in Mark's world things didn't change. In IT things are always changing and if you are comfortable in it, you can move with those changes. I wanted to ask for a refund of sorts, Dad said no as it wasn't the IT school's fault. He was right of course. But that was a whole lot of money not put to good use, and worse yet, Mark felt he had failed.

Mark

Since I seemed to be spinning my wheels looking for a bookkeeping job, my parents thought I should give IT a try. I did all the work, passed all the tests, but couldn't pass the certification test. My instructor told me there were practice certification tests, but they didn't help either. They were nothing like the real test, at least not to me. I was feeling really down when my Mom suggested thinking about Medical Coding.

I was ready to try just about anything. A new Walmart was opening up by us and hiring all sorts of people. So, I decided to give it a try. I failed two of their tests. Talk about feeling like a failure, two college degrees, some IT experience and I can't pass a Walmart test!

I stated writing this memoir to get out some of my frustration. I also started smoking cigars again. I had given up cigarettes when I started dating Claire. She hates smoking. She said she would leave me if I smoked cigarettes. I was afraid to tell her about the cigars. After I burned a hole in my sheets, I gave them up. I did drink too may beers too, but only when I was home and in my bedroom. I would never drink and drive or drink during the day, or ever drink before working. Originally, my Mom didn't say anything about the cigars if I smoked them on the patio. After I smoked in my room and burned a hole in the sheets, I stopped. I stopped flat and haven't smoked them gain.

Mom

I had a girlfriend with a more severely autistic child than Mark. She had also finished college and was at loose ends when she found Medical Coding. This sounded perfect for Mark too; it's a 4-6 months class, on line with a text book and some computer lessons. There are always new diseases, procedures and medicines, but those could be added without too much trouble. Mark has always been able to memorize and recall things with amazing accuracy. He was stumbling with some of the verbiage, and to be honest, I wasn't much help. He asked if he could find a tutor. Sure. Unfortunately she became his new best friend and a household expense for us for the next year. He was afraid to do any of the lessons unless she was right there watching everything. Mark and Claire were planning on getting married that coming October. It was Mark's plan to have the course finished, pass the final test then hopefully get an apprentice type job coding. He passed the course with flying colors. Unfortunately it seems you can't get a job coding without that National Certification. That test is long, 6-8 hours, and they are told that few people pass it the first time. There are practice tests, but he tenses up so that he hasn't done well on them. That has Mark hesitant to take it. It's now been two years....

Mark

I signed up for the on line Medical Coding class. It was offered through a local Community College. It seemed to go pretty well, but I did feel that I wasn't getting some of the information. I asked Mom if we could hire a tutor. I found a great lady with a background in medicine and medical coding who was now a stay at home Mom. We worked really well together the rest of the year; I passed the course with a decent 86% and got a certificate saying I had passed! Unfortunately, you need the National Certification to get a job in coding. I took lots of review tests, but didn't seem to do well. I didn't want to take the real test and fail again. I still haven't taken it.

On October 27th, Claire and I got married. I was stressed that I still was cashiering, and that's rarely a full time job in the grocery business.

I was able to transfer to a store that's close to where we planned on living. We had been engaged for quite a while and knew that we were right for each other. We both take marriage seriously. It was a great day; we got married in my church. It was beautiful, and Claire was a beautiful bride. We had our reception at my parent's country club. That was pretty nice too. I had requested a few Katy Perry songs from the DJ. The young Downs Syndrome girl Claire works with came and she loves Katy Perry. The last song of the evening was Eric Clapton's Wonderful Tonight. People circled around us and clapped. We left for our Honeymoon at Wrightsville Beach. It has become our romantic spot; we went back for our first anniversary.

Mom

It was a beautiful wedding, Claire glowed. Claire had lost her Mom earlier to an awful disease, so she asked me to fill in on some of the Mother of the Bride things. I really appreciated being included. Claire wasn't a bridezilla like you hear about. She knew what she wanted. It was easy and fun to work with her. She was a beautiful bride, the ceremony, everything went smoothly. She has quite a large extended family that has taken us all in, so nice since both Dad and I come from small families, most of our close relatives have died.

Mark

Well, that's about it. Asperger's is a hard thing to live with on a daily basis. I had to spend 20 years of my life not knowing what I had, or why I was different. I keep moving along, but I still don't have a for real job. Claire is beautiful, kind, supportive and understanding. She makes it all worthwhile. I thank God for her being my wife. Now I could just need that career to make my life complete.

Mom

As I said at the beginning, this was a bit of an eye opener. Mark finished putting the memoir together last summer. I had planned on getting it retyped and editing a bit. I haven't changed his text much even though he often uses English as if he isn't a native English speaker. I was hoping to be able to give it to them for a first anniversary gift. I was also hoping that having this published would assuage some of Mark's need for prestige. It's taken me a whole lot longer than I had planned. Through Mark's eyes, we looked like awful parents. We did what we thought was right at the time, and with what information was available at the time. WE can't rewrite things, sorry kiddo. We did our best. I hope you can see that we did all out of love and care for both of our kiddos.

There really were good times in our lives. We have lots of family traditions that are dear to us. We did have fantastic vacations, cruises. As adults, we have taken the kiddos to wander around London for a week while Dad was there on business. Another trip, we had a great week in Dublin, just wandering and sightseeing. We also took Mark and OS and OS's future spouse to Italy for a three city spree, Venice, Florence and Rome. Mark pre booked all the museums that saved us a bunch of time as we didn't have to stand in line. Both kiddos were able financially to go to any college they could get into, both graduated loan free from several colleges. They also got the new car of their choice after the first graduation.

Another surprise to me was several major events in our lives only got a bare mention, or was left out totally.

The first obvious one was 9-11. That was a really scary time for Dad, and me. I did get a call after both towers fell and before all lines were lost, that the whole office was safe and heading to Queens.

OK's wedding got a bare mention. It was quite nice actually. Not the same as Mark's and Claire's. They opted for a justice of the peace ceremony and a huge party. Their only 2 cousins came from Texas for it. We have a bitter sweet picture of all 4 cousins being together the first time as adults. The smiles on bright young faces....hard because their only slightly younger cousin was dead in a year. She had a very aggressive melanoma that she fought long and hard. My sister in law has never been the same.

My Mother, the boys' only remaining Grandparent, passed away a year before he and Claire got married. Mom was 92 and had decided that she was tired of living in a world she didn't understand. She just faded away. Not a mention from Mark.

The event that affected he and Claire the most was Claire's Mom's rather sudden death from something called Lewy Bodies. It's an awful disease that mimics Parkinson's but progresses very quickly and causes debilitating depression. She did get to see her daughter engaged. I was volunteering at school the day she passed. Mark called me in a panic. He was leaving work and going to be with Claire. He asked me the strangest question. He wanted to know how her Mom's death would affect their relationship. My theory of pebble in a pond rings....he was stuck in the "me" ring. I told him what he needed to do was go and be a comfort. She would only be thinking of her Mom, nothing else, for a while. He said ok and hung up.

So, in wrapping up, Mark is our smart, loving, naïve kiddo. He still doesn't have a for real career. Even getting an interview is so different now; you send your resume off into the Ethernet to never know if it's even gotten to the correct place. It frustrates him and us. We are frustrated because we can't help. We can't make things all better.

I do have to add a pet annoyance of mine here. There have to be other resources for employment for the slightly different. WE just can't find them, there seems to be no central clearing place. I get very mad at companies that have big articles in the paper about hiring the autistic, how wonderful of them. Mark wrote letters to the HR people listed in those news articles and heard back from...zero.

I did some thinking a while back and came to a thundering conclusion. Kiddos like Mark would probably learn best in an apprenticeship environment. Maybe class work with an apprenticeship. A century ago, most careers were learning while you minimally earned type situations, or family businesses, farms, weren't they?

So, who's going to jump in this void and create such an environment for our underused, underappreciated different kiddos?

Leah Thompson

BEING ACCEPTED by Claire Thompson 2020

Being accepted takes on many forms
When you're wearing a label, there are lots more storms
People don't realize the pain they create
When making fun of others, they practice
deceit

A person can only withstand so much hate
Before you know it, they make a mistake
So next time you decide to make fun of another,
Reconsider what you're doing, don't be such a bother

There's plenty of ways to get along in this world
Stop hurting your neighbor, this should be the
norm
Follow the example which was set by Christ
He loved everyone, He paid the ultimate price

Think about it sincerely before impulse takes over
Ask yourself twice, "Should I do this to my brother?"
When actions really can speak louder than words
Accepting those around you is not that absurd.

Printed in the United States
by Baker & Taylor Publisher Services